VENTURA COUNTY NEWSPAPERS

Publisher
John Wilcox

Editor
John Irby

Writer
Steve Chawkins

Photo/Graphics Editor
Joe Luper

Director of Photography
Gary Phelps

Photographers
K.C. Alfred, Morris Cohen, Joseph Garcia, Karen Hibdon, David Hartung, Kaison Kim, Chuck Kirman, Ken Koller, Joe Luper, John Mitchell, Victoria Sayer Pearson, Mark Pickering, Kevin Rice, Alisha Semchuck, Ed Skowronski, Jr., Walter Thompson, Scott Weersing

Graphic Artist
John Sherffius

Print Production
Matthew Photographic Services

Cover Photographed by Kevin Rice

ISBN: 1-884850-01-4   FIRST EDITION

Tammy Osburn of Northridge, son Jordan, 18 months, and nephew Jeffrey, 4, try to stay warm after being evacuated from their apartment.

6.6

THE 1994 KILLER QUAKE

VENTURA COUNTY NEWSPAPERS

Moorpark News–Mirror

Simi Valley Enterprise

Star–Free Press

Thousand Oaks News Chronicle

Edited & Designed By
J. BRUCE BAUMANN

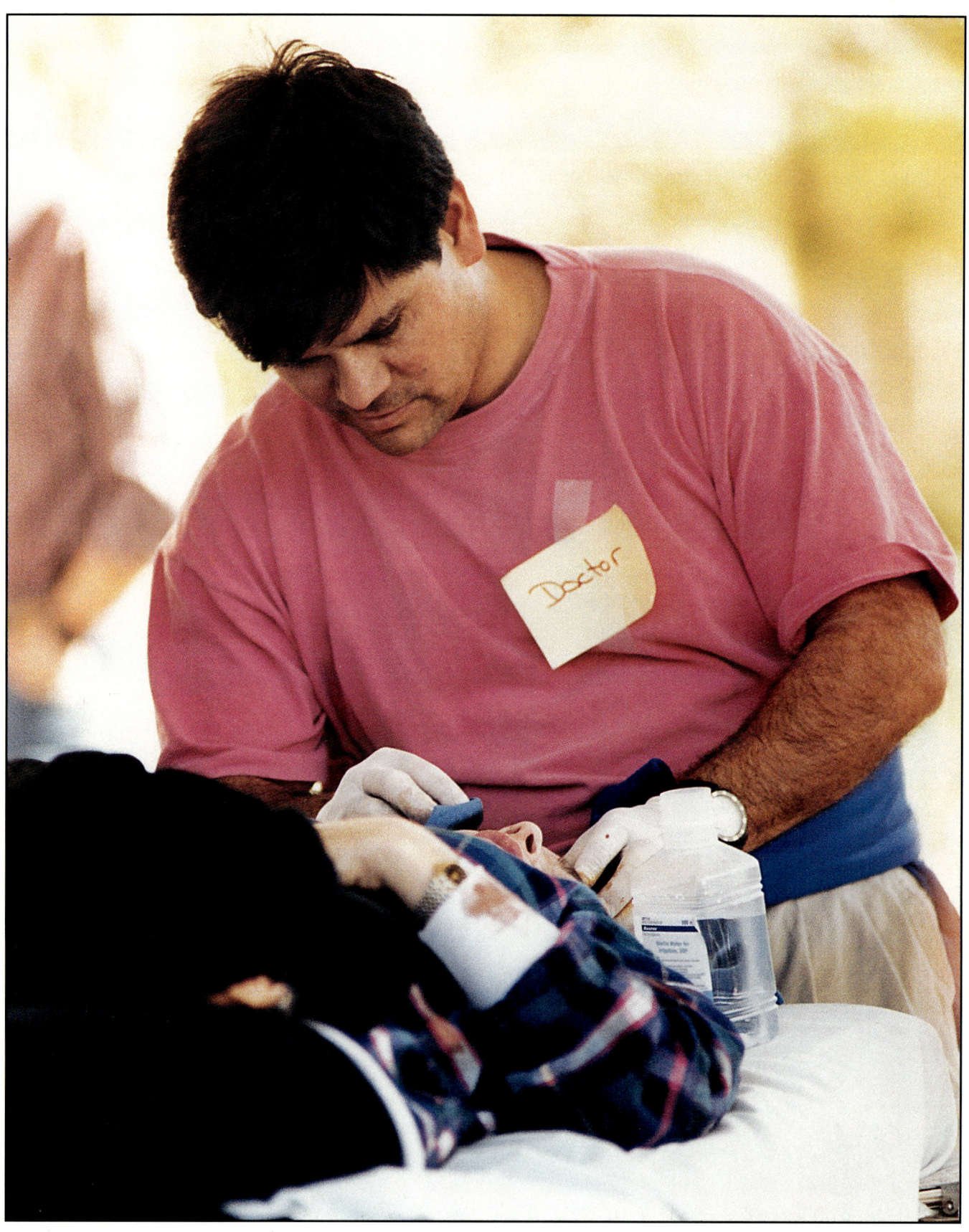

Dr. Richard Wagner works on a patient in front of Simi Valley Hospital. The parking lot was made into a makeshift emergency room to handle the overflow of patients seeking treatment.

About this book

Words, when chosen well, can paint a vivid picture and tell a story.

In 1923, Rudyard Kipling said: "Words are, of course, the most powerful drug used by mankind."

But one picture can be worth a thousand words — and just as effectively tell a story.

What follows is predominately a picture story of the January 1994 earthquake that forever will be etched in the memory of Ventura County residents.

Earthquakes, like wildfires and floods, are natural disasters. Such tragedies are of interest to us all because of the drama and pathos of the event, and because we all want and need the latest news.

At 4:31 a.m. on Monday, Jan. 17, 1994, a 6.6-magnitude earthquake struck like a thief in the night.

It was devastating. While the epicenter was located in the San Fernando Valley, significant damage spread to Ventura County as the tremor fanned out across Southern California.

The hardest hit county areas included Simi Valley and Fillmore. The quake's force and fury left many families homeless. Businesses were forced to close. Critical transportation arteries were severed. Millions were without power and water. More than 60 people were killed throughout Southern California.

It was a disastrous event, but one in which Ventura County Newspapers provided a community service by producing the latest and most complete local news and information in each of our communities.

The Star-Free Press, Thousand Oaks News Chronicle and Simi Valley Enterprise informed the public of those things they needed and wanted to know during the long and tense minutes, hours, and following days of the earthquake.

We continue that commitment of community service with this book, which tells a powerful story of how an earthquake changed and disrupted all of our lives.

This book will take you back in time, and retell the dramatic story of what happened.

Our intent is not to shock you, or vividly remind you of the horror and anguish that took place.

This book will present an historical pictorial, a documentary of the news event as it unfolded — a reminder of nature's sudden power and our need to be prepared for such natural disasters.

Many of the pictures in this book, taken by Ventura County Newspapers' staff photographers, appeared in three "Extra" newspaper editions published within a 24-hour period of the earthquake, or in our newspapers following the quake.

But as you review these strong images one more time, or at other times in the years to come, don't only remember the past, also pledge to be prepared for the future.

— John R. Irby,
Editor, Ventura County Newspapers

The awning and facade of Central Market on Central
Avenue in downtown Fillmore lies in shambles.

That Monday was to be quieter than most.

On Jan. 17, 1994, schools, government offices and many businesses were closed to observe the birthday of the Rev. Martin Luther King Jr.

In Ventura County, a community prayer meeting and march were to be held in Oxnard. The Ventura County Philatelic Society was to hold a stamp auction. And the Center for Counseling and Hypnotherapy in Camarillo was to hold a free lecture called "Stress and Tension: A Cause and an Effect."

For four hours and 31 minutes, the day lived up to its placid promise.

But just over the Santa Susanna Pass and just beyond the grasp of science, it was happening.

Ten miles below the clutter and glitz of the San Fernando Valley, a wordless drama of stress and tension was being played out among vast slabs of rock.

The cause: A release of ancient pressures through fraying faults, prodded by an unseen and unimaginable hand.

The effect: Horror, loss, death, devastation, chaos.

In Los Angeles, scores died, 16 when a three-story apartment building caved in.

Sections of three freeways collapsed. A shopping mall crumbled. Fires spewed from burst gas lines. Thousands of people suddenly joined the ranks of the homeless.

In Ventura County, Fillmore's quaint old downtown erupted in flying brick. Thousands of homes and dozens of businesses in Simi Valley were seriously damaged. A 15-mile oil slick coated the Santa Clara River, the flow from a ruptured pipeline.

Power was cut off. Water aqueducts failed. Telephone service was spotty. The fundamentals could no longer be taken for granted.

Within hours, the terrible phenomenon was named. A legion of stunned scientists and public officials could no more stop the quake or its bruising aftershocks than they could stop a sneeze — but naming a terror has always been the first step toward mastering it.

So it was officially the Northridge earthquake, measuring 6.6 on the Richter scale.

And it was one of the most shattering natural disasters the nation has ever witnessed.

The 30-second jolt will live as long as those who experienced it.

It flipped beefy Jim Chiaro off his bed, wedging him against the wall. Dazed, he pulled himself up and made his way through the blackness of his Simi Valley mobile home.

The retired tool-and-die maker staggered down the suddenly inclined hallway and out the front door. Had he turned into a side room, he would have dropped; the quake had neatly sheared his mobile home's addition off, moving it three or four feet.

Across town, Matthew Weeks was working the night shift at the Pacific Beverage Co. beer warehouse. As the walls started to shake, he loped out the door, barely escaping the thundering crash of 25,000 cases.

"I had Carl Lewis beat," he said.

Throughout the county, couples clung to each other, children cried, terrified dogs barked. Car alarms wailed in chorus.

Sparks flew and a white light flashed in the sky. For a few seconds, power surged wildly through the invisible electronic grid, giving an eerie, bursting quality to hastily switched-on lights.

And then there were none.

Neighbors in bathrobes comforted each other, and checked their houses for gas leaks. They looked up at a sky suddenly alive with constellations, realizing that the only manmade light around was generated by the frail "D" batteries in the flashlight they managed to find in the kitchen drawer.

In Camarillo, 19-year-old Alison Genet was shocked out of bed and into labor. Crouched in a doorway, husband Jason timed her contractions by candlelight before rushing her to St. John's Pleasant Valley Hospital.

Ashley Genet was born under a lone generator-powered lamp at 1:16 p.m. — minutes after an aftershock.

"I can't help wondering how this will affect the person she is," said her amazed father.

In Fillmore, a brick wall crumpled into the windows of a seniors apartment complex. "It sounded like a train hit," said 95-year-old Charlie Myers, who was sleeping with his wife. "I just grabbed ahold of her in the bed and held her until it was all over."

Nobody has complained about that moment not lasting long enough.

"It started out like a regular earthquake with the first jolt," said Bob Sobel, whose Fillmore house lost its chimney. "Then it got stronger and stronger until it felt like the whole house exploded. I thought we were dead."

Miraculously, no one in Ventura County was. At least 798 people stumbled into emergency rooms, most of them cut by flying glass or bruised by falling objects. About 70 were hospitalized.

Some reported chest pains and a few suffered heart attacks. In Santa Paula, a man broke his leg and received other injuries when a car hit him at a darkened intersection. In Oxnard, a woman leaning over a sleeping child had the bone beneath her eyes broken when the child abruptly jerked up.

But for thousands of county residents, the main casualty was confidence. Would the earth suddenly open underfoot? If they left the house, would they return to rubble? If they stayed, would they be flattened? Would their kids be OK?

Jeffrey Mancini, a stock clerk at a Vons supermarket in Thousand Oaks, crawled out of an oozing pile of canned goods and ceiling tiles. His customary California nonchalance about seismic events had vanished.

"I've never been afraid of earthquakes," he said, "but I am now. I just did not want to die in the baby-food aisle."

In the San Fernando Valley, death was just around the corner. As emergency crews fanned through the neighborhoods and poked through the debris for survivors, they would also discover bodies. Sixteen were found in the collapsed Northridge Meadows apartment building.

At least five other people died in smashed houses in Northridge, Studio City, Van Nuys and Sherman Oaks.

A Los Angeles motorcycle officer died in the collapse of a freeway interchange.

Five people died in falls, and one died when a falling microwave oven crushed his head. A 92-year-old woman died in a trailer fire, a 25-year-old man was electrocuted by a downed power line, two people died in traffic accidents, and at least nine suffered fatal heart attacks. More died from other causes.

The tentative total: 61.

Thousands jammed the hospitals. At Cedars Sinai Medical Center, an official wearily talked of "a tidal wave of walking wounded."

Many uninjured people also were among the walking wounded. Some 20,000 valley residents were sleeping in their cars or camping out in parks. Many were unable to re-enter their flooded, burned, collapsed or debris-strewn homes.

Others were unwilling, choosing to rough it outside rather than brace against tremors within. Many of the more than 2,000 aftershocks in the next few days were imperceptible, but at least 32 topped 4.0 — a level sufficient to sway buildings and, for a moment, stop hearts.

While the quake devastated the San Fernando Valley, it merely pulverized parts of Ventura County.

"In dollars and cents, without a question

it will be the most devastating natural disaster that the county has ever witnessed," said Rep. Elton Gallegly, R-Simi Valley.

While the first estimates in any catastrophe are notoriously unreliable, many officials pegged damage in the county at more than $1 billion. That's a small part of the total toll of $15 billion to $30 billion, but still 30 percent more than the county's entire budget.

In Thousand Oaks, the steel ceiling on the city's sleek, 12-year-old library was heaved loose, mangling books, shelves and equipment when it plummeted. Officials said the building could be closed for as long as four months.

Almost all of the luxury homes in the Chanteclair development had their chimneys fall and windows shatter. Some 200 homes were damaged, with five uninhabitable.

Across the county, a gas pipeline exploded beneath Highway 126, carving a crater 15 feet wide and 8 feet deep and shooting out flames five stories high.

Up the Santa Clara River near Newhall, an oil pipeline ruptured, pouring 173,000 gallons of crude into a 15-mile slick.

In Fillmore, bricks cascaded off walls. Walls peeled off of downtown buildings like old circus posters. Dozens of farm workers and their families were asleep in the aging Fillmore Hotel when the exterior walls tumbled outward, crushing a half-dozen cars parked below.

Dozens of shops were ruined. The Central Market was a shambles. A medical clinic — Centro de Salud Familiar de Fillmore — was destroyed. The Saticoy Lemon Association's packing house collapsed, just as packing season was to begin.

The quake in Fillmore damaged 413 buildings, rendering 210 uninhabitable.

Homes were knocked off their foundations. In Simi Valley, people could have used a little more Hollywood. The closest Ventura County community to the quake's epicenter in Los Angeles, it was one of the most brutally hit — and, complained residents, the most overlooked.

"Clinton is talking all about the poor people in L.A.," said Sharon Wright, standing outside what remained of her family's mobile home. "Well, what about the people in Simi Valley?"

Wright, 20, was one of a few dozen people sticking it out at the hard-hit park. They'd been without power, gas, water, or sewage service for three days. Many of the homes were not much more than twisted hunks of metal.

Elsewhere in the city, walls had crumbled and chimneys had toppled. At least 5,000 homes — 12 percent of all those in Simi Valley — were damaged. By the end of the week, 12 commercial buildings, three industrial buildings, three churches, three schools and 622 mobile homes had been condemned.

Water from burst pipes coursed through the East County courthouse, soaking documents and ruining carpeting. The police department was a mess. The roof crashed in at the local movie-theater complex.

"Every business is damaged," said Mike McCaffrey, president of the Simi Valley Chamber of Commerce. "It's just to what degree."

Tents sprouted in yards and parks.

"We slept out front in the camper last night," said Jack Velasquez, a psychiatric technician at Simi Valley Hospital Behavioral Health Center. "I wanted to park it in a field, but my wife is quite nervous and wanted to stay close to the house."

The Velasquezes were among the fortunate.

"Everything inside my house was destroyed," said Teri Johnson, as she tried futilely to make herself and her children feel at home in a Red Cross emergency shelter. "The walls are cracked, the doors won't close. Everything I own is broken and destroyed."

The city's 27 schools were closed all week as building inspectors made their way through. Vandals broke into a few schools, stealing televisions and emergency supplies.

The quake had broken a key water main, but Calleguas Water District officials tapped emergency supplies in the Bard Reservoir. Pressure fell, and water was shut off to as many as 5,000 homes at a time. The water that did flow had to be boiled.

False rumors of an impending water-system breakdown swept the city. Midweek, most of the nervous customers in hour-long lines at a Vons supermarket carried at least one jug of bottled water, as well as bread, peanut butter, toilet paper and other staples.

"I checked it out," confided a woman who was grabbing a cigarette outside the store. "The only thing that can fall on you in there is ceiling tiles."

By Friday, water service was fully restored, mail was delivered again, the Federal Emergency Management Agency had set up a Simi Valley office, and Gov. Pete Wilson had visited, bearing assurances of swift relief.

But even an employee of the Internal Revenue Service had trouble convincing her bosses in San Jose that the people just beyond the San Fernando Valley were also hurting.

"I told them there was damage and they

didn't believe me," said Revenue Officer Leslie Thompson.

They told her they'd send 30 "disaster packets." " I said, '30,000?' They said, 'No. Thirty.' "

After reading copies of local news stories, her supervisors agreed to send 1,000.

Nobody had to be convinced of the anxiety that colored the week, rising with each seismic jolt.

Nobody talked about much else.

"How are you?" asked a woman meeting her friend at a fast-food restaurant in Thousand Oaks.

"Well, the walls are still standing."

Should Tonya Harding go to the Olympics? Was Lorena Bobbitt as crazy as she claimed? And what about those poor souls suffering through that record frigid spell back East?

None of the daily preoccupations mattered. Even Jay Leno's attempts at earthquake humor rang hollow.

"I woke up at 4:30 in the morning, doors slamming, dishes breaking," he told a sparse Tonight Show audience. "I thought, 'How did Shannon Doherty get into my house?' "

How bad was the quake? "The quake was so bad," said Leno, "that Lyle Menendez's toupee ended up on Eric's head."

Even in shaken but relatively undamaged areas like Ventura, Oxnard and Camarillo, few were joking. Many residents had friends and relatives who had suffered heavy damage.

Anil Patel, a Camarillo businessman, had bought three homes in Northridge for family members when they came to the U.S. from India. The quake damaged all three — and, at one point, 32 relatives were gathered under the Patel roof.

Refugees from the valley filled area hotels and restaurants.

"They don't want to sit by the windows," said Maureen Salgado, manager of a Carrows restaurant in Ventura.

As the week wore on, the fear dimmed. After all, the gas stations were pumping, the restaurants were serving, the phones were working, and, in most places, the water was flowing.

But so was the anxiety.

A 5.5 aftershock Monday afternoon underscored it. Lesser aftershocks — two back-to-back 5.1's on Tuesday afternoon, and four on Friday morning greater than 4.0 drove the point home.

As if those weren't enough, "phantom

quakes" — the illusion of earth tremors — also distracted people. "Is that me or is it real?" was a refrain that punctuated the week.

For most, neither answer was entirely comforting.

"At first, the quake is frightening and all," said Marc Subido, a Moorpark College engineering student living in Simi Valley with his wife and three children. "But then there's this anxiety; you just don't know what's going to happen."

"We still have the tent up," he said, "just in case."

By week's end, it was clear that the systems in place to deal with cataclysm had functioned comparatively well.
"I don't think there was a single surprise in this whole earthquake," said Sheriff Larry Carpenter. "It's things we've studied, been in seminars about, but I guess it's like a war: Until you've been in it, you don't know what it is."

But — unlike a full-dress earthquake exercise conducted by local agencies last October — this was no drill.

By 5:15 a.m, the Emergency Operations Center in the basement of the County Government Center was in full swing.

Law enforcement agencies across the county were ready to roll. In Simi Valley, firefighters started cruising the streets, realizing that people with dead phones couldn't call in to report a blaze.

The Red Cross was preparing to truck blankets, food, cots and workers to four emergency shelters it would open in Simi Valley, Fillmore and Piru. The agency would at times house more than 800 families and dish out thousands of meals.

Emergency crews from Southern California Edison also were working before dawn.

Still dealing with repairs from last fall's firestorms, company officials predicted power might not be restored for 72 hours. But, partly because of the experience gained in that disaster, workers managed to channel electricity to most areas of Ventura and Santa Barbara counties in just 10 hours.

"We were ready for something like this," said crew supervisor Don Kaeser.

Government response was also brisk. On Thursday, the Federal Emergency Management Agency opened offices in Simi Valley and Fillmore. Residents waiting to apply for low-interest loans had to wait as long as two or three hours — but it took 12 days for FEMA to open shop after the 1989 San Francisco quake.

If officialdom worked in harmony, there were still plenty of disquieting notes.

Reports of price-gouging for bottled water

Mark Pickering

An earthquake refugee in the Royal High School gymnasium is among those taking advantage of the Red Cross evacuation center set up in the gym.

and other basics surfaced in Simi Valley. Traffic from Ventura County to Los Angeles was smooth, but many motorists were staying home; commuters were girding for trips tenser, longer, and more grinding than usual.

After riot, fire, and recession, the quake would for some be the final insult.

"If I didn't own my own home," said Jeff Siminofsky, of Moorpark, "I'd be on the highway out."

And uncomfortable questions remained about just what this quake was.

Its vertical motion was unusual. So was its violence, which scientists described as extraordinary, even for a 6.6 temblor. Seismologists also weren't sure whether it originated on the Oak Ridge fault, which traverses Ventura County, or on a previously unidentified fault in the San Fernando Valley.

What they did know struck the most dis-

quieting chord of all:

This wasn't the Big One.

The projected 8.3-magnitude monster — invoked so often it has verged into myth — is more than 60 percent likely within 25 years, according to some scientists.

"We're getting very close," said Tom Henyey, director of the Southern California Earthquake Center.

But as the earth stopped moving and the final chunks of plaster stopped falling, the Big One was only a grim possibility. The immediate demands were to clean up, calm down, and help out.

"We're all pitching in," said Sister Guadalupe, a nun from the San Salvador Mission in Piru as she sorted through stacks of donated clothes and food at a Red Cross shelter. "People even suffering through this are helping one another."

— *Steve Chawkins*

This overpass on Interstate 5, where it crosses The Old Road near Santa Clarita, was destroyed.

Kevin Rice

Two cars lie on The Old Road near Santa Clarita after plunging from the crumbled overpass of Interstate 5, which was destroyed during the earthquake.

A truck is stranded on the edge of the severed overpass of Interstate 5, where it crosses The Old Road near Santa Clarita. The overpass was destroyed during the earthquake.

Wendall Hildebrandt, Ventura County Sheriff's deputy, looks over damage at the Fillmore Hotel.

Mark Pickeri[n]

Spectators gather to look at the rubble created by the collapse of the Northridge Fashion
Center shopping mall parking structure.

Mark Pickering

A San Fernando Valley road shows cracks from the 6.6 quake.

K.C. Alfred

Blockbuster Video manager Anita Troup cleans up videos and other merchandise amid shattered window glass at the business in the Mountain Gate Shopping Center in Simi Valley.

Pacific Beverage Company employee Craig Carr, right, climbs onto a mountain of beer created when 25,000 cases tumbled down during the earthquake.

The awnings and bricks from several Fillmore business district store fronts cover the sidewalk on Central Avenue.

Store owner Harnek Singh Behniwal, right, inspects the damage to his Central Market in Fillmore.

Ed Skowronski

The Interstate 5 overpass near The Old Road in Santa Clarita was ripped apart by the earthquake.

Scott Weersing

A van was crushed and totaled on Fillmore Street outside the Fillmore Hotel when bricks fell on it.

Ed Kulik, Thousand Oaks building inspector, checks out damage at the Thousand Oaks Library. The library was opened in the late 1970s, and closed by the quake.

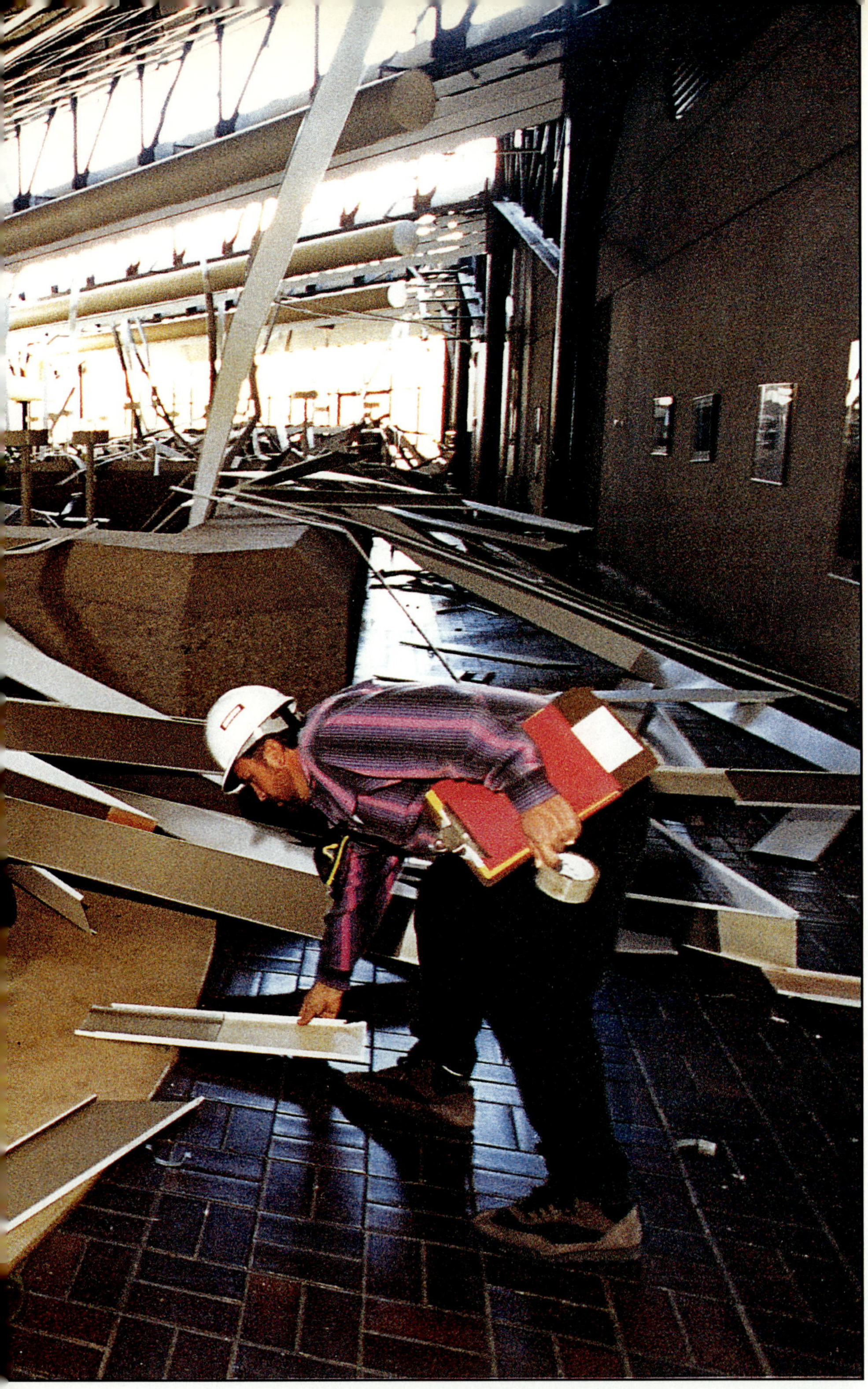

Joseph Garcia

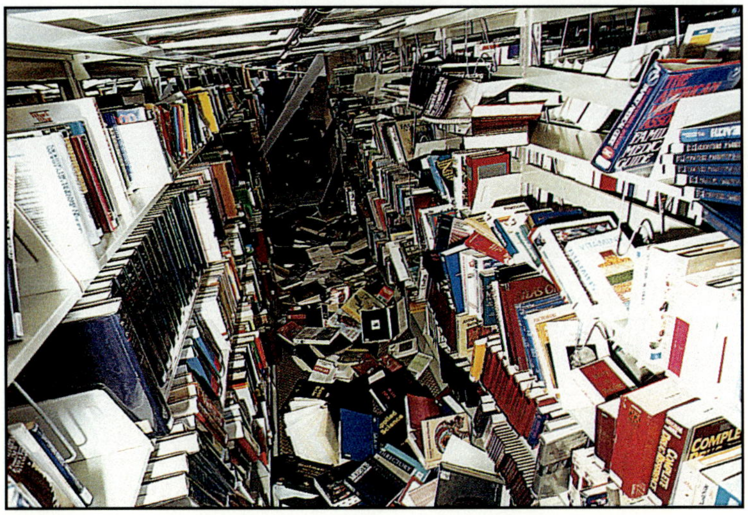

Thousands of books were thrown from their shelves during the 6.6 earthquake, and several books were damaged by fire sprinklers.

Mark Pickering

Sulfuric acid spilled from this derailed freight train in the San Fernando Valley.

Mark Pickering

Workers use a crane as they try to clear the tracks of a freight train that derailed during the earthquake. Sulfuric acid was spilled as several tanker cars overturned.

Walter Thompson

A worker moves stock in Erica's Baby Buggy store
in Simi Valley following the quake.

A mannequin fell through the front window of a Fillmore store on
Central Avenue and Sespe Road.

The Pencil House in the historic Bottle Village in Simi Valley is in ruins after the earthquake. Several other structures in the complex survived the earthquake.

A D.A.R.E. sign encouraging kids to keep off drugs is overshadowed by the damage to Kaiser Permanente Hospital in Granada Hills.

Ed Skowronski Jr.

A fire rages just after Monday's 6.6 quake near the intersection of Ladonia Street and Corpus Christi Avenue in Simi Valley.

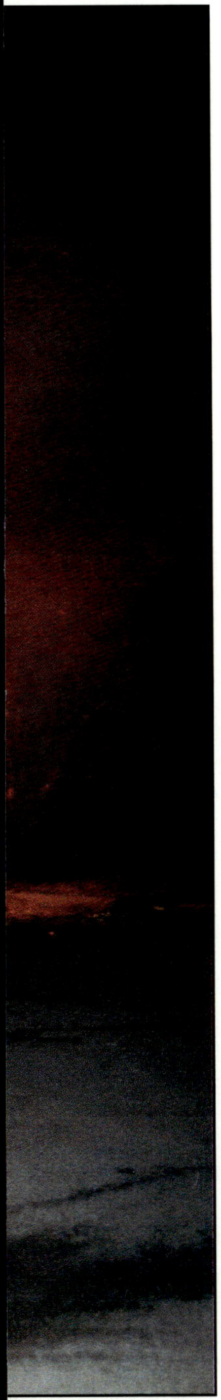

Scoot Weersing

A natural gas explosion scooped out a 15-foot-deep crater in the eastbound lanes of Highway 126 east of Fillmore.

Kathy Martinez's home fell off its foundation and was declared off limits by Fillmore city officials.

A two-story home in Fillmore fell to the ground as the wood foundation failed, making the front door only five feet high.

Scott Weersing

Kelly Gomez, who lives next door, stands outside the home of her sister, Kathy Martinez, whose home fell off its foundation and was declared off limits by Fillmore city officials.

Mark Pickering

Firefighters and emergency personnel remove a man who was trapped beneath the rubble of a three-level parking structure at the Northridge Fashion Center shopping mall after the facility collapsed. Workers labored for hours to extricate the victim.

Scott Weersing

Mike Quintanilla, owner of Mike's Services on Central Avenue in Fillmore, talks with building inspectors and fire department personnel who told him he could not enter his business because it was unsafe.

Joe Luper

A worker in Albertson's on Avenida de Los Arboles in Thousand Oaks
cleans up items that fell off the shelves.

Businesses in Simi Valley were hit hard by the quake. Workers try to pick up the pieces in this beauty salon.

Simi Valley's Mann Theater was heavily damaged.

Several automobiles were crushed by brick that fell from the second floor of the Fillmore Hotel during the 6.6 temblor.

Rooms on the second floor of the Fillmore Hotel are exposed after the brick walls fell during the earthquake.

Walter Thompson

A Simi Valley businessman removes broken glass from Erica's Baby Buggy store in Simi Valley following the quake.

Kaison Kim

Cynthia Hawker, left, and her husband, Brent, clean up the remains of coffee mugs their Simi Valley business sells to the armed forces.

Chuck Kirman

Ventura County building inspectors Tom Melugin
and Trini Mendoza look at building damage in
downtown Fillmore.

A man walks by the Giant Video store on the corner of Santa Clara Avenue and Saratoga Street in Fillmore where an aftershock caused a wall (far right) to fall onto the sidewalk.

Mobile homes and cars were destroyed by earthquake-caused fire in the El Dorado Mobile Home Estates in Fillmore.

A trailer home on Rindge View Way in the Friendly Village Park of Simi Valley has its front porch wrecked.

Ted Pearce helps his mother-in-law, Virginia Griffin, out of her trailer home after it fell three feet. Griffin and her husband, Frank, live in the Friendly Village Park in Simi Valley. Of 220 trailer homes in the park only 33 did not fall.

Ed Galik of Preferred Glass in Simi Valley carries sheets of plywood that were used to board up windows at a Sears outlet store. The store roof also collapsed.

Kathryn Scroggin, principal, and Denise Vale, assistant principal, at Simi Valley High School, discuss the collapsed overhang on the campus' D building. Simi Valley High was among the schools that were closed for an extended period of time.

Water from a storage tank on the hill behind the Simi Valley home of Fred and Debbie Alfono rushed down the slope, flattened the wall and roared through the house on the way to the street.

K.C. Alfred

Paula Fisher, right, and neighbor Dianne Alfred check out Fisher's knocked down backyard wall on Fullbroke Drive in Thousand Oaks.

Dennis Parker stands next to an oil skimmer that is being used to clean the Santa Clara River in an area about four miles east of Piru. The spill was caused by the quake.

Kaison Kim

California
Conservation Corps
members attempt
to clean up the oil
spill on the banks
of the Santa Clara
River north of Piru.

Kevin Rice

Ed Skowronski, Jr.

A gas main explosion in Granada
Hills destroyed the road surface
and burned down several homes.

David Hartung

Carol Anderson helps with the cleanup activity at C & C Custom Ceramics in Simi Valley.

The Northridge Fashion Center collapsed during the quake, trapping a man who was operating a sweeper.

Mark Pickering

Joey Fama, 13, slogs through the mud filling the Simi Valley home of cousins Fred and Debbie Alfono. The mud on the walls indicates the high water mark of the flood that raged through the home.

Heline Goftschalk and husband, David, try to make it through the kitchen in their Vaccarat Street home in Thousand Oaks.

Victims of the
quake are treated
at Fillmore's San
Cayento School
triage center.

Scott Weersing

Alisha Semchuck

Luis Crous and other residents of the Simi Valley Rehabilitation and Nursing
Center were evacuated to the parking lot after the earthquake. The center was
declared unsafe.

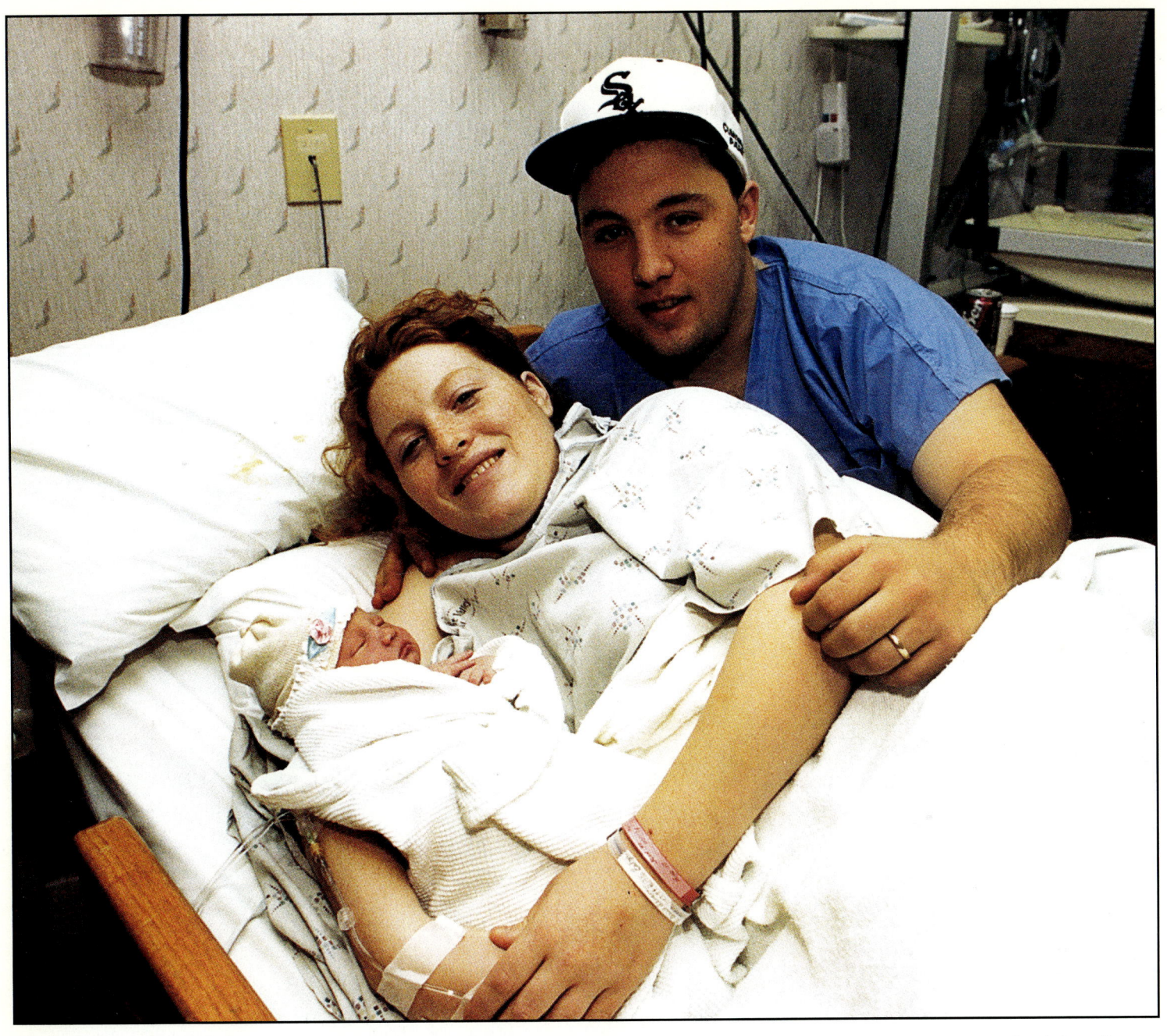

Ashley Genet was born at Pleasant Valley Hospital in Camarillo, the day of the earthquake. Her parents, Alison and Jason Genet, live in Camarillo.

People lined up at a Simi Valley Vons store to buy supplies after the quake. Water, ice and batteries were among the most requested items.

Royal High basketball player David Pulsipher helps his sister, Becky, prepare lunch at the evacuation center at Royal High.

Ramee Hijaz sets up an outdoor market on High Street in Moorpark after the quake closed his Mayflower Market.

Joseph Garcia

David Faria, 7, Simi Valley, helps deliver drinking water to a local
resident after the Southern California Water Company made spring
water available to earthquake victims without water. Water was
made available at the Amtrak Metrolink station off Los Angeles
Avenue in Simi Valley.

David Hartung

Seismology professor Gerry Simila, of California State University, Northridge, monitors seismic activity from his Westlake Village home.

Kaison Kim

Workers tried to beat the rain in Fillmore, at Holy
Family Home Peace, where a chimney collapsed leav-
ing a gaping hole in the roof.

Victoria Sayer Pearson

Fillmore kindergartner Giselle Hurtado, 5, was still feeling a little unsettled a week after the 6.6 quake.

Kevin Rice

Rosalba Lopez cooks breakfast for her family on a makeshift outdoor grill next to their home in Piru. Gas and electricity were not restored for several days after the earthquake.

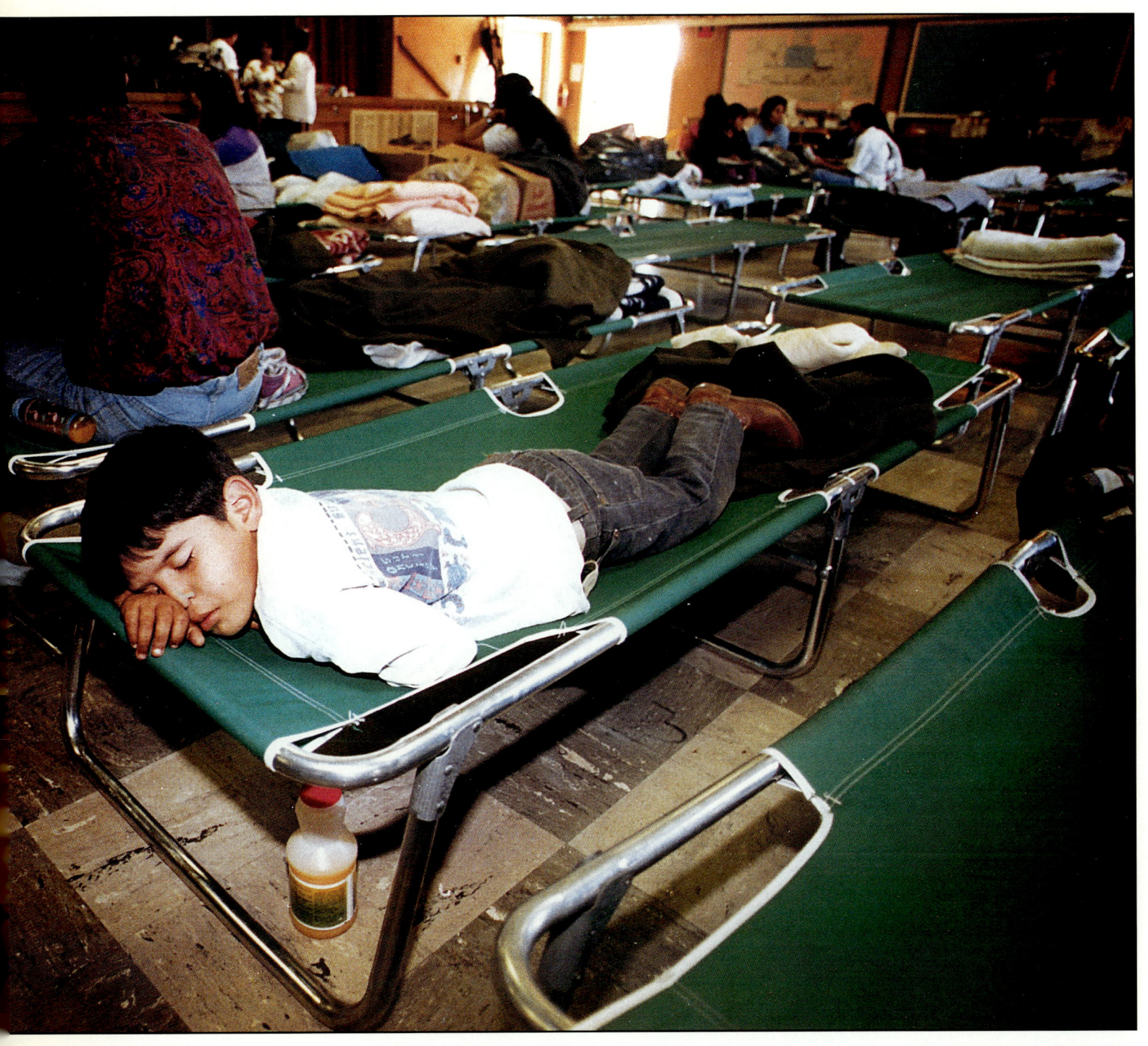

A young boy sleeps soundly in the cafeteria at San Cayento School in Fillmore where the Red Cross established a disaster center for displaced residents.

Families frightened by aftershocks moved out to their front lawns in Fillmore. Most believe that the Big One is yet to come.